THE NEW EQUINOX
THE BRITISH JOURNAL OF MAGICK

A reprint of selected articles from *The New Equinox: The British Journal of Magick* (1980-1981), originally written by Jim Lees and edited Carol A. Smith, compiled here by Cath Thompson for Hadean Press.

Hadean Press
BM Box 6176
London
WC1N 3XX

www.hadeanpress.com

THE NEW EQUINOX
THE BRITISH JOURNAL OF MAGICK

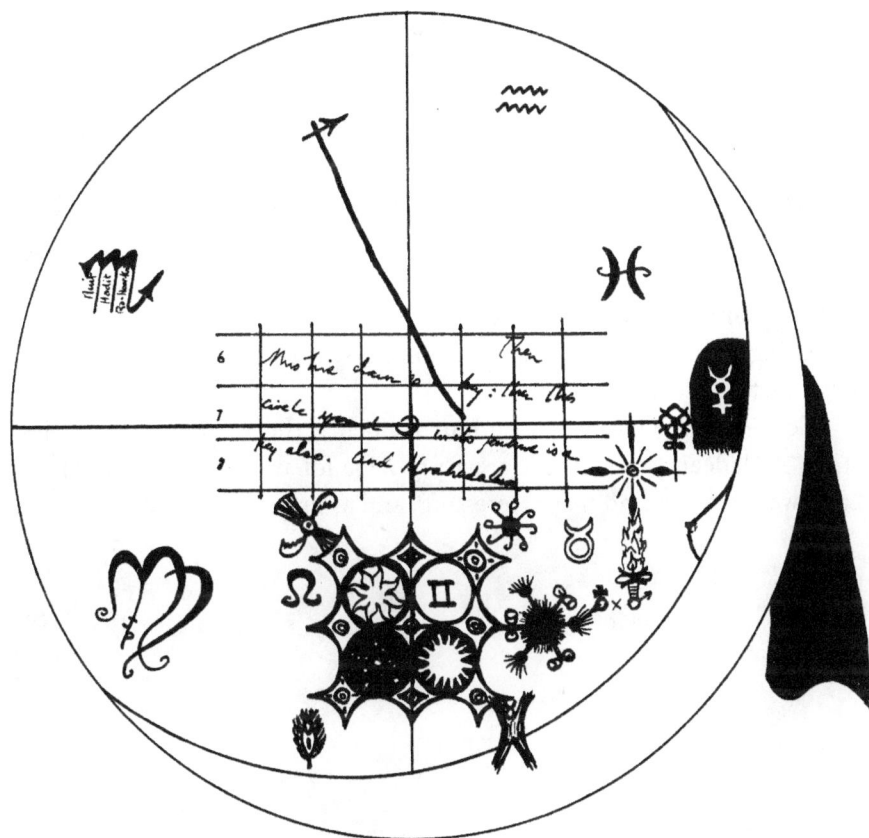

INTRODUCED BY
CATH THOMPSON

Publisher's Note

These documents represent an important part of the recent development of Western Magick in general, and in particular of a specific brand of English Magick, that of the English Qaballa. They offer a glimpse at the magickal activity occurring in the English Midlands at the time, and record the changing of the editorship from Ray Sherwin to James Lees, who took over *The New Equinox* in 1980.

Articles have been selected for their relevance to the EQ, and in them you will find a record of how this system developed, as well as an autobiographical account of the man who discovered the "order & value of the English Alphabet". While the EQ is wholly a product of *The Book of the Law*, you do not need to be a Thelemite to appreciate the material presented here.

We have done our very best to scan these from the original issues without causing them damage. They are not in all cases perfect scans, but the text and diagrams are entirely legible and the original page numbers, advertisements, and editorials have been left intact.

Considering what a tremendous influence the English Qaballa had on the formation of Hadean Press, it is a great privilege for us to bring this work back into print, and we hope you find it as interesting, and as useful, as we do.

Erzebet & Dis
Hadean Press

CONTENTS

INTRODUCTION

THE WORRYING FACT of a genuine Qaballa in English was first put to the occult reading public in 1979, in the Editorial of the final issue of Ray Sherwin's periodical *The New Equinox*. The "order & value of the English Alphabet," predicted in *Liber AL vel Legis*, had been obtained in the English Midlands by a magickian named James Lees in November 1976, and with the members of his occult group he had researched, experimented, and proved the new system to the point where the first conclusions and propositions could be shared.

Lees took over the publication of *The New Equinox* with the subtitle "British Journal of Magick" and published several articles about the English Qaballa in 1980-81, in five issues. He employed a variety of pseudonyms intended to compliment members of his group in a privately shared joke (including that of his co-editor, Carol Smith). The writings were published under different bylines, because as Lees later explained they were written for those people, and not by them; adding that any buffoon who doubts this has only to compare the literary style of the different pieces, and hunt for more writings by any of the other individuals named.

At the time there was just a small ripple of interest among the post-Crowley generation of occultists. A few years later Jake Stratton-Kent continued publication of *The Equinox*, dropping the word "New" on the grounds that *The Equinox* was by now fully established, and adding the subtitle "British Journal of Thelema". With his group in the West Country he continued to research and experiment and publish results in eight further issues of the magazine, and both he and Lees maintained websites on the Internet from its earliest beginnings in the 1990's, where the first articles and much subsequent work were published.

At the turn of the century English Qaballa had achieved some notoriety despite the lack of information regarding later development of the system that proved its initiatory significance, which only became available after Lees' death in 2015. By then, Hadean Press had published Stratton-Kent's *The Serpent Tongue* which explored the application of EQ to Goetia, as well as the last three issues of the BJoT, and it seemed obvious that future E. Qaballistic titles should be on the Hadean list. After a meeting between myself, Stratton-Kent and Hadean Press, it was agreed to reprint the EQ articles from TNE/BJM and a selection of writings from BJoT in a separate publication.

THE REPRINTING OF articles from *The New Equinox: British Journal of Magick* gives me the opportunity to right a serious wrong, and pay a tribute long overdue. In the mid 1980's Carol Smith was wrongly credited with having discovered the Qaballistic order and value of the English Alphabet – an error which she herself sought to correct, having no desire to stake any part of such a claim. James Lees found the Qaballistic Key and wrote all of the articles given here – which were edited for publication by Carol Smith.

None of it would have appeared in print without Carol Smith's dedication and sheer hard work. She created the five editions of TNE/BJM, directed and produced them.

In the early 1980's there were no computers with word processing facilities presenting automatic paragraph formatting, page layout and design at the press of a button or two, and more fonts than you can shake a stick at. There were no domestic printers either; there were offices with electric typewriters and photocopying machines and two O...A...A... members employed as secretaries with a bit of spare time at lunch. Then there were scissors and craft knives and pots of glue, for "cut and paste" was exactly that, with positioning guidelines drawn in blue pencil which the black and white photocopiers couldn't see, and white correcting fluid to hide the edges. Finally there were sheets of rub-on transfers of decorative edges and borders, and a selection of headline-sized typefaces. Carol somehow brought all of these together and produced the magazines which introduced the English Qaballa to the world. She also dealt with the printers; and she looked after the marketing, processing orders from all around the globe. Her achievement is of inestimable value, and I thank her unreservedly for it.

JAKE STRATTON-KENT was introduced to English Qaballa and its discoverer, Jim Lees, by way of *The New Equinox: British Journal of Magick* which had been published by Ray Sherwin before he passed the title and format to Lees; Stratton-Kent had declined the editorship but wrote to Lees, and they met in 1980. Both magicians were running small occult groups, and there was an exchange of visits between the Midlands and the South-West, and sharing of English Qaballistic research and magickal-astrological theory.

One of the major contributors to both groups was the late Trevor Langford (Brother Daedelus), a computer programmer of exceptional talent, who wrote the first English Qaballistic evaluation software. He worked with Lees on the research into astrologically timed rituals until the late 1980's, when the Tamworth group was dissolved and Lees went into retirement, handing the magazine format on to Stratton-Kent along with certain research documents and ritual paraphernalia; Langford also went to the West Country, and worked for a number of years with Stratton-Kent and his group. They took up Lees' early work and pushed forward the research into the English Qaballa on their own. Results were written up for publication in the magazine, renamed "The British Journal of Thelema". Some of the earliest material was derived from Lees' notebooks and appeared under the byline "LEO", but over the eleven volumes of the BJoT we can trace the development and refining of a ceremonial system rooted in E. Qaballistic astro-philosophy and entwined with Goetic magick to a very detailed extent.

Stratton-Kent's researches into the English Qaballa reflect the breadth of his academic foundation and his experience as a ritualist, and may be described as dealing with practical applications of E. Qaballistic theory in a precisely focussed fashion. He demonstrates the ease with which the English Qaballa dovetails into other systems, with ritual formats and procedures drawn from sources diverse as Aleister Crowley and Dr. Dee and incorporating elements from the earliest Grimoire traditions through to 20th Century chaos magic. More importantly, Stratton-Kent dares to step beyond the usual indoctrinations, armed with the truth of pure number in his own mother tongue, and proposes new ways of doing old (and probably worn stale by custom) spells and incantations.

I AM PARTICULARLY pleased to be involved with the current project. In the 1980's occultism was a basis for an undercover kind of lifestyle without fashionable accessories, a far cry from the present climate of academic indulgence and establishment-led tolerance; and only just emerging from the shadow cast by the Golden Dawn and the "Great Revival" to formulate new answers to the old questions. English Qaballa has not only withstood the tests of Time, but expanded from the first hypotheses into a complete coherent and harmonious initiatory system of alpha-numeric symbol correspondences, a viable alternative to the non-English systems which have dominated occult publication for decades. The reproduction of its advent and early development should therefore be of interest to a new generation of enquiring minds as well as to those who may be renewing an old familiarity.

Cath Thompson
literary executor for James Lees
December 2017

Volume 4 No. 3. 1979.

Morton Press

Ed. Ray Sherwin

EDITORIAL

THE NEW EQUINOX VOL IV NO 3. ● MORTON PR.

The past twelve months have been unfortunate ones for occult magazines. First SOTHIS joined Sirius B in obscurity, then the MONOLITH toppled and recently has come the news that GNOSTICA, even with the weight of the mighy Llewelyn behind it, is also dead.

Saddest of all from my point of view is that THE NEW EQUINOX is doomed to follow the example of those erstwhile worthy competitors and this issue is the last I shall be producing.

Single-handed, under various editorial pseudonyms, I have been producing TNE since Novenmber 1976 and I feel that I have now fulfilled what I set out to do. It may be that at some time in the future I will take up the task once more but I would prefer that someone else take up the challenge. I therefore invite anyone with a serious interest in editing and publishing THE NEW EQUINOX to make an appointment to see me so that I can offer the benefit of my experience and the unpublished works in my collection . Interested parties should phone 097-666-9886 during normal office hours.

It would be impossible for me to write individually to the many individuals who have given their assistance and encouragement over the past few years. To them I offer my sincere thanks. Subscribers who are left with monies outstanding are requested to write to me at the usual address informing me whether they would prefer a cash refund or MORTON PRESS books to the same value. To all subscribers I offer my thanks for their continued support.

In the way of an alternative to THE NEW EQUINOX I recommend the NEWAEON NEWSLETTER, see ads in previous issues, as the only Thelemic magazine remaining.

Now to business: I have refrained in previous issues from commenting on the absurdities of the so-called "EQUINOX VOL V" published by Thelema. Whereas I find it hitherto unproved that Mickey Mouse wears a Marcello Motta watch I find the spumiferous spilth of his editorial comments criminally contradictory to the Law of Thelema. His instruction to buy only books he has produced himself is fine for people confined to Roy Plumley's desert island where only two books are allowed but does he expect Thelemites not so marooned to make do with the Commentaries on AL and his own drivelling comment on Liber 231? We can't wait for ever Mr Motta. If you're intending to publish more Crowley material we suggest you get on with it instead of pretending to initiate gullibe young people into the organisation which you improperly call the A..A.. Better still, we suggest you start a trucking business and leave the occult to the people whose business it is.

Finally, I've given over most of this issue to two sections of THE TEMPLE OF SOLOMON THE KING. I had originally hoped to include the entire 800 page work as a serial but this will not now happen unless my offer is taken up.

In the meanwhile, I hope the sections included here will be of benefit to those people who do not own THE EQUINOX.

Herewith, T.N.E. IV:3.

THE QABALAH OF AL.

I have in my possession an eight page document which was sent to me some months ago for inclusion in TNE. Unfortunatley there is insufficient space to include the whole of the article but the actual working of the method is too interesting to omit. The following passage is quoted from the original. If you'd like to contact the authors of the document please let me know.

In late November 1976 a small group of occultists who had been working on Crowley's Book of the Law for many years were studying verse 76 of Chapter Two:- "4, 6, 3, 8, ABK 24 ALGMOR3 YX 24 89 RPSTOVAL. What meaneth this O Prophet" etc. Between us we had three calculators and several good mathematical brains. We were working with a simple numerical attribution of the alphabet. Independantly II:76 was added up by several people and the number 286 obtained. 286 factorises into 13x22 and 11x26. 22 is the number of letters in the Hebrew alphabet and 26 the number of letters in the English alphabet. Thus 286 is the link between the Hebrew and English alphabets. Hebrew is a qabalistic language, 11 is a number of vital importance in the Book of the Law. 11 is the key to the alteration of the English aiphabet to give a perfect qabalistic system. Thus A = 1, then it is left and 11 letters counted and the next numbered 2 and so on -

When Z is reached start counting again so that the alphabet is continuous. 11 fits perfectly - a previously numbered letter is never reached until all are numbered. The final order and value of the English alphabet is

```
a  l  w  h  s  d  o  z  k  v  g  r  c  n  y  j  u  f  q  b  m  x  i  t  e  p
1  2  3  4  5 .............................................26
```

Now the really strange part of all this is that 286, the number which started it all, has no basis in fact - II:76 adds up to 388. Yet this number frequently occured on calculators and was given as the answer by manual adding as well.

We did not discover or invent the English Qabalah, we were in the right place at the right time when it was uncovered by the Gods.

Volume 5 Part 1. 1980.

Editorial

&

The Qaballa of AL by Carol A. Smith
(aka Jim Lees)

editorial

We are delighted to announce the arrival of The New Equinox – The British Journal of Magick – an occult quarterly review of all aspects of Magick & Thelema. We intend to continue the best aspects of T.N.E. plus hitherto privately circulated material available only to initiates.

This issue contains an unusual article on English Qaballa based on information contained in the Apocryphon of AL, as well as a tongue-in-cheek approach to the sacred muchroom by Brother Pan, and the "Citnalta Working" an example of ritual magick at its most hilarious.

Ray Sherwin, the previous editor of T.N.E., hallowed be his name, has contributed an excellent article on sigilisation, and there is a personal and sensitive view from a candidate to a ritual order.

The editor thanks you for your continuing support.

Jim Lees

3

I'm sure all readers of The New Equinox will be as delighted as I am that the breach has been filled and that the magazine survives.

To the best of my knowledge future issues of TNE will be continuing the tradition started in Vol IV: 1 : carrying previously unpublished Crowley articles and acting as a forum for Thelemites and other magicians.

The new Editor also has a great deal of information of his own resulting from many years of experience in the subject, all of which I look forward to seeing in print.

I wish him and his colleagues the greatest success with their new venture. All power to The New Equinox. With your support it will live forever.

4

THE QABALLA OF AL

by Carol A. Smith

It will take as long as the history of mankind to write a commentary to AL because the history of mankind is the commentary. What we are seeking to achieve is to explain some of the ways in which the Qaballa is being used, but first we will discuss the parallels and divergences between the English Qaballa and previously accepted methods of analysis.

Aleister Crowley gave us Liber AL; he solved the first half of the equation, but he could not resist trying to solve the second. This resulted in attempts to translate English words into Hebrew, Greek, Egyptian, Chaldean, and other languages in order to make some sense of Liber AL. In a previous incarnation he had interfered as a desperate magician and wrested the Enochian System, stillborn, from the bosom of the Goddess. In this Aeon the gods wreaked their vengeance on him in an all too obvious manner for his opportunism.

Liber AL, if it is a hieratic text, must have a qaballa in the language in which it was written or it simply cannot be counted as as a hieratic work. We are presenting to Thelemites the Qaballa of AL in English, - we can do no more. It will then be up to them whether they "go down the tubes" of Set or go forward into the New Aeon armed with a magic citadel, the power of which the world has not known for many aeons.

5

Magick is a complete, coherent and logical system requiring no faith but work, its Qaballa requires the same attribute.

In our last article we gave the English Qaballa and a rudimentary explanation of a few of its numbers, and it was our original intention to leave it at that. However, we realised that it could take years for the reader to work out the Keys, so we decided to speed up the process by giving some of the English Qaballistic magical system of AL within the Law of Thelema. (The information in this article is up to the Neophyte grade of our order).

Magick is based on AL and AL is based on number, the number 11 to be precise, which gives, as explained in our previous article, the following English Qaballistic values:-

A	L	W	H	S	D	O	Z	K	V	G	R	C
1	2	3	4	5	6	7	8	9	10	11	12	13

N	Y	J	U	F	Q	B	M	X	I	T	E	P
14	15	16	17	18	19	20	21	22	23	24	25	26

We repeat - no qaballa can be used to interpret a hieratic book unless it is in the language of that book!

We will begin by comparing some of the conclusions of other Thelemites with those given by this Qaballa.

6

For instance, Aleister Crowley said the "ORDEAL X" was the ordeal of the "BEAST", and indeed

BEAST = 75 = "ORDEAL X".

The number 75 being a union of the root numbers of Nuit - 7 and Hadit - 5.

ORDEALS = 58 = HADIT, X = 22.

ORDEAL (53) + X (22) = 75.

The Hadit particle suffers the agony of crucifixion and wins the ordeal of the 22nd path of fear to give the total initiation of the beast. In Geburah matter is changed to spirit and vice-versa, only the purified Hadit particle can get through, as it is the infinitely small particle of matter. Being NOT it can pass through the pylons of the 5th sphere.

HADIT = 58 = ZODIAC = HOUSE,

an important fact which will be referred to later.

HADIT = HOUSE and 418 is the name of "His house". 418 is among other things the total value of II 75 - "Aye! Listen to the numbers & the words:" we know 75 = BEAST. II 75 is followed by the universal formula of II 76.

Crowley was Ankh-af-na-Khonsu the Priest of the Princes, the scribe of the Book of the Law. "The pen" adds up to 118 as does Ankh-af-na-Khonsu and Princes. Thus we have the identification of Crowley with the scribe. Interestingly "The Hand" adds up to 78 which is the same as Nuit.

There has been much discussion of 93. The empirical meaning of 93 in the English Qaballa is "the formula of unity through denial" exemplified by the astrological sign SCORPIO = 93. It is the formula of the ORIGINAL = 93 and DIVIDE = 93.

The Goddess divided for love's sake symbolised by the time of year Sun in Scorpio.

Among the Celtic peoples of Norther Europe there has always been the tradition of Halloween fires. This date does not coincide with any of the four great turning points of the Solar year, nor with any specific agricultural event or season. Sir James Frazer in the "Golden Bough" can postulate no convincing reason for this date. There is evidence that the Celts dated their new year from the 1st November. A new sacred fire was lit and all others rekindled from it. Stones thrown on to the Halloween fire will by their position and condition the next day tell the fortune of those who threw them. Around this time the English celebrate an obscure Plot, which failed, by an obscure 17th century dissident, Guy Fawkes, with unfailing enthusiasm. This smacks rather of an excuse to light fires come what may, to reinforce an earlier and deeper memory. The Christians incorporated the feast of Saturnalia into their calendar in the same way, utilising an already present tradition.

The great fires of Europe are lit to commemorate the DNA memory of the beginning.
        FIRE = 78 = NUIT creating TIME = 93.
That the universe will end the same way it began is cosmological truth, and is exemplified in the fourth house of the Zodiac "The end of things", the sign
        CANCER = 78 = NUIT = FIRE.
Cancer is the sign of the mother and the period of the greatest night. As it is said "The manifestation of Nuit is at AN END. The end of the Goddess AN = 15 as 78 = 7 + 8 = 15. The end is the fourth house of the Zodiac - Cancer. This digression into the Zodiac is quite valid in Class A - See "The treasure house of images."

8

In the Book of the Law themes are followed throughout all three chapters in linked verses. The links may be a key number like 93 or a word like "Thee" or even the device of studying the same number verse in all three chapters. The puzzle of the key number 718 is an example of how the numerical values link with the text to give blinding insights into the nature of Man and the Universe.

With the number 718 we are at variance with Aleister Crowley on logical grounds. For those who would dispute this let them turn to the expanded commentary on III 19 for a treatise of mind-blowing contortions and fiddling. To explain AL using words like XAIPE, AXPICTA, CTHAH, and CTAYPOS etc. is as silly as converting Hebrew words into Chinese to illuminate the Qaballa of Genesis. No, let us use the method of Science to illuminate the Aims of Religion.

> I 19 "O azure lidded woman, bend upon them".

> II 19 "Is a god to live in a dog? No — but the highest are of us."

> III 19 "That stele they shall call the abomination of desolation, count well its & it shall be to you as 718".

The Goddess says "I give certainty not faith while in life." All previous religions have demanded faith from their followers:- You must believe because. In the New Aeon the Goddess Nuit furnishes proof, gives certainty; there is no call for faith, no need of because. Proof gives certainty. III 19 furnishes that proof.

Ra-Hoor-Khuit is a God of war and vengeance. Hadit gives the knowledge of death, therefore the stele is the stele of the Goddess Nuit. Initiates know that the "abomination of desolation" is space. In II 19 we get "The highest are of us". Wherever one is in the universe the sky or space is the highest phenomena. The sky is the azure lidded one bending upon us, as shown in the stele of revealing. Any other stele must exist within space, within her. "O azure-lidded woman bend upon them" is a key to the proof of the certainty of Nuit.

AZURE-LIDDED WOMAN has the initials A.L.W. ALW are the first three letters of the alphabet when arranged qaballistically, (see above) which would indicate that the phrase has more than ordinary significance.

"AZURE-LIDDED" interested Crowley in that it has the initials "AL" and has eleven letters. He suspected that it had a deeper meaning, but although he tried for many years, off and on, he never succeeded in elucidating it.

If we take the phrase "Azure-Lidded Woman" the initials A. L. W. have the numerical values 1. 2. 3. In the English Qaballa, the phrase "I am Nuit" adds up to 123 as does "Revealing" and "Threefold". This is dramatic proof that the azure lidded one is indeed the Goddess of infinite space - Nuit. Azure-Lidded in our Qaballa adds up to 131 which is also the value of "UNIVERSE".

Now to the injunction to "Count well its name" i.e. the name of the stele - of space - of Nuit - of the azure-lidded one. This requirement is also fulfilled by our Qaballa. If every letter of the one word is added to every letter of the other word and the whole is totalled it comes to - 718! It is indeed counted

10

well.

```
        A  =   1          L  =   2
        Z  =   8          I  =  23
        U  =  17          D  =   6
        R  =  12          D  =   6
        E  =  25          E  =  25
                          D  =   6
```

```
A                Z           U            R            E
1 +   2 (L)      8 +   2     17 +   2     12 +   2     25 +   2
1 +  23 (I)      8 +  23     17 +  23     12 +  23     25 +  23
1 +   6 (D)      8 +   6     17 +   6     12 +   6     25 +   6
1 +   6 (D)      8 +   6     17 +   6     12 +   6     25 +   6
1 +  25 (E)      8 +  25     17 +  25     12 +  25     25 +  25
1 +   6 (D)      8 +   6     17 +   6     12 +   6     25 +   6
_____        _____     _____      _____      _____
   74              116         170          140          218

                              =
                             718
```

The general formula is, sum of first word x number
of letters in 2nd word + sum of letters in 2nd word
x number of letters in 1st word.

(Incidentally, if the same counting process is applied
to SUN-MIDNIGHT the total is 666, and there are other
significant phrases which similarly give key numbers).

The stele "The abomination of desolation" is the sky
Goddess, the highest.
Verse III 20 following is "Why, because of the fall
of because that he is not there again." Nuit causes
the fall of because through certainty. The proof is
written in her stele, the unity - 1 - of the Goddess
Nuit 78 - 7 (1) 8.

11

The reader may well be a little bewildered by these details and wonder what relevance the Qaballa has to him, and what purpose it serves. It is written in AL - "The book of the Law is written and concealed." AL is concealed in its Qaballa of 11. In expounding a few, a very few, of the numerical puzzles of AL it is our desire to stimulate Thelemites to investigate further this magick of the New Aeon. There is little purpose to be served in trying to sharpen the old rusty swords of magicks long dead, but Thelemites as Siegried must forge the new sword of Thelema from the concealed law, our law that is the joy of the world, and then and only then will this regenerate the world. "The little world my sister, the sister and bride of On of the God that is all and in none by the power of eleven." The power of eleven that when applied to the English alphabet reveals AL.

As we said in the beginning it is not our purpose to try and lead Thelemites but to freely give them the keys that they may see for themselves. The task that has been laid before us is to simply reveal the Qaballa before the Eighties are upon us. It is up to Thelemites to use their discrimination - for in the beginning did not our Goddess teach discrimination?

There is no place for faith in Thelema. If your Holy Guardian Angel grips you and drives you onward, as he did us, then yours will be the Ordeal X, and should you win then certainty will be thine. The certainty of Nuit and victory will be thine, and joy of earth, ever unto her. Aye, ever unto her.

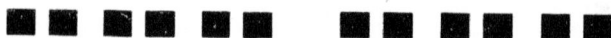

■■ ■■ ■■ ■■ ■■ ■■

12

Volume 5 Part 2. 1980.

Editorial

&

The Abyss by John Deacon
(aka James Lees)

(This article is not E. Qaballistic but autobiographical, being a partial account
of James Lees' earlier Magickal endeavours.)

&

The War-Engine of Thelema by Stefan Dajnowicz
(aka James Lees)

editorial

The editors of The New Equinox, The British Journal of Magick, wish all Thelemites all over the world a beastly Crowleymas (October 12th), and success in the Great Work.

The reception given to the first edition of TNE/BJM has been magnificent. We thank all those who have written, and promise that we will answer all of your letters as soon as possible. Please have patience; the Thelemic year is a busy one – we went to press between the Supreme Ritual and the Feast of Jupiter.

We trust you will enjoy this issue; some material has had to be held over till next time due to lack of space (next issue out a little before the solstice so that distribution does not get tangled up with Christmas post – published December 11th), however, we have published another major article on the English Qaballa. We searched our souls before we put in the Golden Verses of Pythagoras – translated by Aleister Crowley – but since this material is from a private collection and previously unpublished, we decided it was valid to include it.

Jim Lees & Carol A. Smith – Co-Editors

It is the intention of this Magazine to publish in plain language the secrets of The Rosy Cross, The Blazing Star, The Holy Grail, The Unity of The Goddess and The Horizontal and Vertical Components of Alchemy and their relationships to the English Qaballa, the central secret of magick.

    🜨 107 71(8) ☉ 01* 777/813 ♂♀ 15th June 1980

Individuals and/or groups objecting to the exposition of these mysteries are invited to put their cases to the Editor. Should there be valid reasons as to why these subjects should not be revealed then the Editor will refrain from publishing.

We would remind these groups and individuals that the year is 1980 e.v.

THE NEW EQUINOX

Available from Kaaba Publications

12A Albert Road, Tamworth, Staffs, England

Price £1.50 + 20p post & packing (US & Canada $5.)

Yearly subscription £6.00 post free (U.K. only).

The Abyss

by John Deacon

"As a process of integration qaballistic meditation is by far the best method for people of the West". This is a statement we meet again and again in occult publications, but what are the results to be expected from such work? In this article I intend to relate my own experiences of fifteen years study of Qaballa from a Thelemic point of view. I will keep the technical side of the method to a minimum and concentrate on the psychological effects of prolonged working with The Tree of Life and the magical powers the student may expect as he is initiated by the spheres on the Tree of Life. The Authorities I used were Dione Fortune's "Mystical Qaballa" for theory and Israel Regardie's "Middle Pillar" for practical instruction.

I read and re-read these two works, lived ate and breathed them, until they were imprinted upon my psyche.

"The Middle Pillar", for those who are not familiar with the book, is a series of practical instructions which are an expansion of the 22 papers of the Order of The Golden Dawn.

It is recommended that one keeps a Diary of all the work done and any results noticed. This is a requirement of all initiatory magical work. It allows one to earth the magical experiences and inhibits them from running around in one's mind afterwards. This earthing is important as it stops one drifting between the planes and becoming ineffectual on all of them. It is also fascinating to look back and see how one has changed as the magical work proceeds.

One begins by balancing one's psyche by the daily practice of the "Lesser Ritual of the Pentagram". The method is in "The Middle Pillar" and in many other occult books. The effect of continued practice of the pentagram is to integrate and balance the mind emotionally and intellectually. Without this preliminary work, exposing the mind to the power of the middle pillar could be dangerous and cause unbalancing obsessions.

The ground plan of Qaballa is the Tree of Life. This has been described severally as, a map of the soul, of the universe and of the self. From the magician's point of view it is a map of experience that tells him where he is at any given point and is invaluable as an aid to stop him going completely mad as the mystical–magical process begins to cause stresses in his psyche.

The Middle Pillar instructs one to perform a simple 6 – 3 – 6 – 3 breathing exercise while relaxing and visualizing the spheres on the middle pillar starting with Kether above the head. The results experienced by the breathing exercises are very interesting as the amount of time given to them is increased. One lies relaxed feet together concentrating on getting the rythm right and keeping it that way. Quite suddenly one is aware of a gentle rippling sensation that according to Regardie should play around the abdomen but in my experience covered the whole of my body. This is followed by a feeling that one is a source of enourmous power, or gigantic storage battery of energy. This happens quite suddenly and is apt to disorientate one somewhat causing the heart to beat faster and thus destroying the concentration. However with repeated experiments one "gets used" to this sudden influx of power and learns to relax through it. With continued effort one reaches a stage where one is so relaxed that if one were required to move suddenly it would be found impossible to move at all! This point is followed by a feeling of falling away and deeper relaxation. I felt somewhat afraid at this point as I felt I was losing control of things so I decided to stop at that point of relaxation and negin to work upon the middle pillar of The Tree of Life.

I visualized gently the Sphere of Light above my head and went through the attributes of Kether – all very gentle. After about four attempts I found I could see it in my mind's eye and I vibrated the God–name Eheieh powerfully. I found that the name vibrated through my whole body causing every nerve to tingle – a very pleasant sensation. Then suddenly, as if a light of immense brilliance had been turned on, there it was, a brilliant white Sun above my head – it was really there! a white sun radiating love light and wisdom into my mind. It was really there, it was more real than I was. It took me several experiments to become

50

accustomed to this power. I found that as the centre above my head lit up, the Malkuth centre between the ankles lit up by reflex. The experience was delightful it was pure ecstacy.

At this point my eagerness was such that I suffered from "The Lust of Result" and it was many months before I could awaken the centre again. During this period one has just got to slog on with the exercise not wanting anything from it – just do it.

Eventually the light above the head came back and I drew it down to the Daath centre at the nape of the neck. It is very difficult to describe these experiences in terms that can be understood by one who has not undertaken the work. Upon hitting the Daath Centre the Yesod Sphere exploded in sympathy. My attention was drawn to this centre, the effects were most interesting. There was a feeling at the base of my spine of great relaxation – of falling – then suddenly of immense pulsating power, like a snake uncoiling and with its uncoiling tremendous pulsating energy, like orgasm. The experience was pure delight and far superceded any other pleasure I had ever experienced in my life.

With repeated experiments I learned not to "grab at" the pleasure experienced but to ignore it and get on with the work.

As I got used to handling the power generated by these exercises I began to examine the symbols associated with the centres while performing the meditation. During normal consciousness the symbols on the Tree of Life appear dead and un- connected but during the hyperconscious states of meditation the symbols become living entities. One is aware of Malkuth as oneself. The enormous power generated makes one negative to it and the attitude taken up automatically is a feminine experience. One literally changes sex and takes on a feminine Goddess form so that the energy flows through the Malkuth personality unimpeded. This is not a contrived experience but a natural reaction to the power invoked. One becomes negative to receive the divine bridegroom of Tiphareth. I found that when the divine bridegroom of Tiphareth descended to Yesod and the bride ascended and united with the divine male it caused every other male and female deity to unite on the whole Tree of Life causing a state of orgasmic bliss that cannot be compared with anything in mundane experience.

During the whole of this period my mundane consciousness and personality were undergoing great changes caused by this massive influx of power. It is said that it is important to keep the two states separate and now I learned why! When one is practising as intensly as I was during this period if one so much as thinks of the centres they awaken and this can be very inconvenient in ordinary life.

Although during the meditations I experienced the great bliss of transcendental vision my mundane personality was under unbelievable stresses. I had invoked the powers of the universe which are damn near perfect into a system — myself — which was far from perfect. I was full of conditioning and ideas that simply were not true. The whole of my mind's complexes were turned upside down. I went mad but managed to appear sane to the rest of the world. The stress my mind was under defies imagination. I continued the work remorselessly. I wanted to know the truth and nothing else mattered. During the crisis period in meditation I had come to a point again and again but was afraid to cross. Those who know this state will recognise it for what it is — The Abyss.

I had reached the Tiphareth centre. I had lain in the harmony of eternity and drunk of the dew of immortality and by God now I was paying for it by mental torture. Again and again in meditation I reached the edge of the abyss and again and again I drew back in terror, my consciousness on the edge of annihilation. It felt as if were I to go over the edge I would be destroyed forever. Each time I returned to normal consciousness I hated myself for my weakness and vowed countless times that next time I would let it happen, I would go and die, and each time my vow was broken my humilation was insufferable. Finally I decided that it did not really matter anyway because sooner or later I was going to die so why not now as in a few years time. I prepared myself by the pentagram and hexagram and took up the breathing after an hour and a half of meditation gradually taking myself through Godname after Godname. I reached the edge of the abyss. I was filled with terror again, the kind of terror that one can never get used to. I backed away from the edge again and again but I was determined that this was the time and I would not return empty handed. I looked into the inexpressable horror, called out the name of my Angel and let go. I was thrown, literally thrown, from one state to another. I was suddenly beyond time and space, the past and future were one. I knew all my past lives and all future lives, my brain full as if it was burning up, such was the nuclear blast of ecstacy that filled it. In that moment I was eternity and knew all

53

to existence, man was supreme and it that moment I could see it all.

How much time I existed across the Abyss I do not know. I was catapulted back as fast as I had entered it. I was aware that if I had remained a moment longer my brain would have burned up. It was strange but I could actually smell a strong scent of burning in my physical nostrils.

I returned with an awareness of my destiny, of my past and future, and was confident that in that mind blasting experience I had seen God. After this experience it became much easier to integrate my psyche. Half the rubbish had been burned out by the experience. I felt childlike. Though I felt I had to relearn everything, I knew that everything I had been taught by parents, environment, even experience was rubbish because it was all orientated from one lifetime's point of view, but I lived forever and I knew it. I was as a child - a child of eternity and I had to learn the rules. I thought at the time that this would take forever but was amazed to find that the "rules" of existence were natural, only man lives by unnatural rules.

The law of existence is "Do what thou wilt" and "love is the law, love under will". Find your true will, lay your life and sanity at the feet of the Goddess and find,   There is no God but Man.

The war-engine of Thelema

STEFAN DAJNOWICZ

We are entering a critical period in the evolution
of mankind. The principles that have guided us and
the institutions that have guarded us for the last
2,000 years can be seen crumbling everywhere.

Since Crowley received the book Al in 1904 whole
countries have changed their ways of existence.
Russia and China aware that the old ways could not
survive returned to the primitive fundamentalism
of the communist state. The banding together of
the masses against a real or imaginary enemy and
living out and existing in a seige situation. The
death of religion is occurring throughout the world;
for make no mistake, Hinduism and Islam are losing
their grip upon the peoples they have ruled, even
as the Christian era is crumbling. It is only a
seige mentality of a people that would return it
to Christianity, Islam or Hinduism. The fear of
praeternational influences threatening a nation
causes its people to band together under what should
be a non power based institution - their religion,
but they only find themselves being manipulated by
a Godless state. The theoretical end to such a
situation i.e. where a nation's religion fails to

59

sustain its people through a national identity crisis, war is needed with another country to re-affirm its national identity. These are the ways of the old aeon and they are defunct, the new Aeon is with us and its principles as written in the Book of the Law and illustrated by nature are irrefutable. We are on the Threshold of a new beginning when mankind will be truly emancipated into the Cosmos, no longer a mere curiosity to travellers in the body of our Lady of the Stars, but civilized members of her life. The principles of Thelema are being integrated into humanity's thought stream. Changes are occurring on the astral plane, devastating because mankind THINKS IT CAN RESIST the changes required by the Gods. One of these changes is indicated by the loss of identity caused by unemployment in the Western World of an ever increasing number of workers - the anthill no longer needs them. The powers of Al, of the aeon, are making people look inside themselves for an identity. Instead of being labelled by what one does, it is what one is that will matter and those that fail to find themselves will find that not only are they redundant as workers but as souls as well. The Book of the Law is implacable on this matter.

In Thelema is a philosophy that will guide us for the next 2,000 years. Do what thou wilt shall be the whole of the law, and with its Qaballa an affirmation of the direct nature of the message from the Gods that liber Al is. A message that can stand up to all the modern methods of computer analysis affirming the transcendental nature of its transmitters.

60

Magick is based on AL and AL is based on number, the number 11 to be precise, which gives, as explained in our previous article, the following English Qaballistic values:-

A	L	W	H	S	D	O	Z	K	V	G	R	C
1	2	3	4	5	6	7	8	9	10	11	12	13

N	Y	J	U	F	Q	B	M	X	I	T	E	P
14	15	16	17	18	19	20	21	22	23	24	25	26

No man could have written liber Al: its Qaballa proves this beyond any doubt . For a human being to have contrived Al he would have had to live for several thousand years, a being all powerful, capable of directing a language completely, he must do this and more. Finally he must communicate in some unimaginable way a book - a cipher functioning on all qaballistic levels - a perfect Qaballa concealing and revealing the nature of man and the universe with the magick of the Aeon that controls them. He must write in "whiter words" the truth that is neither word nor number but the truth that exists between them, that is the truth that exists within the Thelemite.

It is my understanding that Thelema is the laws of nature and that man has always been obedient to those laws, even though it appears he disobeys at every opportunity. NATURE = 93. E.Q. Man has always been ruled by expediency and in whose hands but the Gods is the cause of man's dilemma?

Everything in the universe is as it should be. The whole of mankind is under the impression that there is something wrong with the world - a world directed by the same power that controlled man to the extent of directing totally the form of several languages, culminating in the English language and perpetuating their message aeon after aeon, eternally bridging the gap between planes.

- and man has the audacity to think that he rings the changes in the world.

"Do what thou wilt shall be the whole of the law", but just find your true will and when you do you will find that your true will is divine. The important point is that man has always obeyed his true unconscious will, the conflict has only been caused by man's inability to bridge the planes of consciousness and live in harmony with his true will. Make no mistake his actions would not change, but he would be enlightened and at least know the reasons for his actions. The fact the man's future can be predicted by astrology and other divinatory systems proves that the will of man is the will of God. The statement that the will of man is the will of God does not in one iota change man's experience, the break between planes causes the illusion of "Free will". The reason that the Gods gave man this illusion is simply part of the divine dance of creation, a cosmic belly laugh at man's expense. For a spiritual inter incarnating being that man is, all things in spiritual experience are just plain fun. Seen from the standpoint of the eternal spirit all human joys and woes are just the spices of existence. What would you do if you

62

lived forever and could do anything? You would create the universe and populate it. You would create the world and man so that you could experience all the combinations of exist nce and this is what the Gods did.

All mystics from the beginning have said that mankind is one and we are just that, different aspects of the one being created for love's sake with the illusion of individual will - for love's sake or if you like - for fun - can you hear Pan's laughter yet? If you can't I'll explain the cosmic joke a little more. The English language is the 93 current and its use has the effect of a mantra, the mantra of the 93 current - The law of Thelema - Whatever state or country accepts the English language as its first language will inevitably become Thelemic. The whole language from its structure onwards is the supreme Thelemic Spell. The whole Thelemic ethos is built into the structure of our language, and, MARK CAREFULLY, the whole world will share our language in Time because the language is of the nature of TIME for is not TIME = 93.

The language born out of the bosom of Nuit the Hieratic language of the new aeon is the English language - your heritage from the Gods.

THE ENGLISH QABALLA

The foundation of our belief in the English language is the provable fact that an hieratic text exists in English - Liber Al Vel Legis - The Book of the Law.

Below are the statements made in Al concerning the Qaballa with our interpretation given by the side. I must stress that the Qaballa was obtained without any recourse to this type of logical process.

1:36   My scribe Ankh Af Na Khonsu.The Priest of the Princes shall not in one letter change this book.

This statement is taken literally : that one letter only must not be changed.
But what letter?

1:54 Change not so much as the style of A letter.

This leads us to believe that the letter mentioned in 1:36 is A. The rest must be changed, but how?

1:60 My number is eleven as all their numbers who are of us.

Of them? All their words must be of them and as they are Gods then their words must be "living" words that somehow obey the number 11.

2:16 Thus 11 as my bride is 11.

A reiteration of the above statement.

2:54 The letters? Change them not in style or value.
2:55 Thou shalt obtain the order and value of the English Alphabet.

It is stated in Al "The stops as thou wilt", which means that one could read verses 54 and 55 right through.

If one reads this in English it does not make sense. How can one by not altering the book get the order and value of the English alphabet? We have to look closely at the word NOT which in Hebrew is אל or

64

LA. It has again the Hebrew Qaballistic value of
eleven! This is further emphasised by the eleven
letters in the statement Thou shalt obtain the order
and value of the English Alphabet. To summarise
the whole procedure, the letter A must not be
changed in style or value while all the rest may
be changed by the number eleven, which as shown
in our previous article gives the following values-

A	L	W	H	S	D	O	Z	K	V	G	R	C
1	2	3	4	5	6	7	8	9	10	11	12	13

N	Y	J	U	F	Q	B	M	X	I	T	E	P
14	15	16	17	18	19	20	21	22	23	24	25	26

As may be seen, there is a marked resemblance
between many of the letters and numbers, but this
is not important for the moment.

I have never been satisfied with Crowley's explanation of the spelling of magick and I do not think
he was satisfied with it either. Let us consider
the Qaballistic values of our subject MAGICK, our
supreme Goddess NUIT and our politics, OZ.

$$\text{MAGICK} = 78$$
$$\text{NUIT} = 78$$
$$\text{OZ} = 7 + 8.$$

It is written in Al that 8 = 80: and 418 all equal
nothing or therefore 78 = 7 to $\propto$ and 7 = 0 in E. Q.
Therefore magick is the philosophy of the infinite
zero. Nuit is the Goddess of infinite zero (Space
= 70 = 00 or $\propto$) and OZ is its politics.

A considerable number of words were checked using
this Qaballa until we were convinced that it was

65

indeed genuine and that the interrelationships did work, better than in the Hebrew or any previous qaballistic text.

It soon became obvious that we had to work out the values of every word, sentence, paragraph and verse of Liber Al and work statistically from there. This work occupied the year 1977. A Sepher* Sephiroth was prepared and a number chosen to be examined in minute detail. The number chosen was that of Thelema in Greek – 93. Below are listed every known 93 in Liber Al.

I.3.   My ecstacy is <u>in yours</u> [93]

I.9.   and behold my light shed <u>over you</u> [93]

I.21.   There is <u>no other</u> god than me. [93]

I.25.   <u>Divide</u> add multiply and understand. [93]

I.51.   <u>Be goodly</u> therefore, <u>dress ye</u> all in fine ap [93] [93]

I.61.   But whoso gives one particle of dust shall all in <u>that hour</u>. [93]

I.62   At all my meetings <u>with you</u>. [93]

II.5.   Behold: the rituals of old <u>time</u> are black. [93]
            Then shall this knowledge <u>go aright</u>. [93]

---

* "The Apocryphon of Al" shortly to be published by Kaaba Publications, it will contain the whole text of Liber Al with the numerical values, and a Sepher Sephiroth of all words and significant phrases.

66

II.15.   For I am perfect being not.
                                    93

II.22.   Fear not that any God shall deny thee for this.
                                                            93

II.26.   In my coiling there is joy.
                      93

II.39.   A feast for Tahuti and the child of the prophet.
                            93

II.58.   Deem not of change.
                        93

II.61.   There is a light before thine eyes.
                      93

II.66.   Thrill with the joy of life.
                                    93

II.68.   Hold up thyself.
                      93

II.69.   What do I feel.
                      93

II.75.   Aye listen to the numbers and the words.
                  93

II.78.   Lift up thyself lift up thyself.
                      93   93

III.11.   From the ill ordered house thou shalt thyself.
                          93   93

III.14.   Ye shall see that hour.
                          93

III.23.   Soften and smooth down.
                  93

III.24.   The Host of heaven.
                  93

III.34.   and blessing no longer be poured.
                                          93

III.37.   Unity uttermost showed.
                  93

III.38.   I have made a secret door
                  93

III.42.   The ordeals thou shalt oversee thyself.
                                              93

III.44.   Let her be shameless before all men.
                          93

67

```
                                        93
III.47.    but always with the original in the writing
           the Beast.

                                        93
III.55.    Be utterly despised among you
                              93
III.60.    There is no law beyond do what thou wilt.
                    93
III.75.    The ending of the words is the word Abrahada.
```

The problem then was what was the empirical meaning of 93? To answer this question we will have to refer back to two other statements in Al. II 32 Also reason is a lie for there is a factor infinite and unknown and all their words are SKEW WISE.

The word SKEW is the pointer, it has a value of 42 which is the same value as STAR. "He shall bring the Glory of the STARS into the hearts of men." At the end of II 55 it states "Thou shalt find NEW symbols to attribute them unto. NEW = 42 = STAR = SKEW.

Are we to assume then that the stars are directly related to the system, that the words of the Gods are not subject to reason but to the Stars? ZODIAC = 58 = HADIT, but for our purposes 93 is the number we are interested in. The Zodiacal sign Scorpio the house of Death is equal to 93. It will be found in The Treasure House of Images Liber 393 that Scorpio is Unity through Denial.

Then 93 is the formula of Unity through Denial – The formula of Life and Death.

All the various methods of working using the old Hebrew Qaballa have proved to be equally valid in working with the English Qaballa. Here are some other methods of working which may be applied to the text and give coherent magickal results.

THE PILLARS

This is where a number has a 1 either side of it, as in 1_11, 1_21, 1_31, etc. This number indicates a power acting in balanced manifestation: thus 121 is balanced duality as expressed in CAPRICORN, DELICIOUS, RAPTUROUS, REJOICE, which all add up to 121.

131. Here 3 = AL in balanced manifestation in words such as UNIVERSE, SUPREME, SERPENT.

141 (4 elements) in the words ELEMENTS, CONTINUOUS, and BEAUTEOUS.

151 (Geburah) EIGHTEEN, CERTAINTY, LIGHTENING.

161 (Chesed) REMEMBER, REVERENCE, SWEETNESSES.

There is no 171 in Liber Al as 7 = 0 and is the root number of Our Lady of the Stars, and 7 being the infinite zero cannot be expressed.

The number 181 is expressed in the word UNUTTERABLE and since according to Liber Al 8:80:418 = 0, balanced zero cannot be borne, and hence

        181 = UNUTTERABLE
            (utter same root as uterus)
representing a word that cannot be spoken.

191 9 is Yesod: illusion. Illusion cannot be in balanced manifestation: if it were it would not

These are numbers ending in 8. These represent Archetypal concepts in that they are the ground rules for one eternity.

18 (Kether) = CALL, GO. As Crowley said one's only function is to go.

28 (Chochmah) WORD, WE, IS. In the beginning was the word and the word was with GOD and the word was God to quote an old Aeon script. Then if God and the word exist, God is giving rise to WE.

38 (Binah) AIWASS, ARE, JOY. This proves two things: one, that Aiwass is the three in one divinity and that the Vision of Sorrow of Binah is truly a mask for the Vision of Joy.

48 BODY, CHILD, DOVE, GOODLY. 4 is Chesed: the divine plan. God made man in his own image BODY - CHILD. The Dove was sent out from the Ark in search of land or order - Chesed. GOODLY - conforming to the Chesedic plan.

58 HADIT, HERU, HOUSE, ORDEALS, SIGNS. 5 is Geburah and the root number of Hadit - the smallest particle. The Hadit particle that is nowhere found yet is the house of being and contains within itself all Karma i.e. ORDEALS and SIGNS.

68 (Tiphareth) CHANGE, JESUS, CHOSEN, LIFE, PALACE, PROUD. The sixth sphere is the pivot of the Tree

70

of Life. It is the sphere of the old Aeon God, Jesus: it is the first manifestation of <u>life</u> which provokes CHANGE. Tiphareth is also the <u>PALACE</u> of the King.   The vice of Tiphareth is <u>PRIDE</u>.

78 7the great mystic magickal number. NUIT, THEE, MANTRA'S, TRUE, LITHE, FIRE.
7 = 0 8 =   78 is infinite nothing.

88 CIRCLE, ECSTACY, MASTER, BLESSED.

98 DELICACY, FAILURE, TIMES, LIFTED.

108 FORTRESS, GARMENT, MISTAKE, REFUCE, VISIBLE.

118 ANKH-AF-NA-KHONSU, MIRACULOUS PRINCES, PURPOSE.

128 BES-NA-MAUT, PRECIOUS, RIGHTEOUS, WRITTEN.

138 ENEMIES, VENGEANCE.

148 INNOCENCE, MEETINGS, WORSHIPPERS.

158 CENTURIES.

168 FORTH-SPEAKER.

178 THELEMITES, COMPLEMENT.

We have deliberately kept to a minimum the numbers studied. The idea being to give magickians some ideas to work on within their terms of reference so that they may more quickly accept the INCREDIBLE RELIABILITY of the English Qaballa.

In future articles I am going to discuss the practical aspects of The Qaballa, the rituals of The rituals of the Stars, as it is said "He shall bring the Glory of The Stars into the hearts of men." These rites have remained secret for centuries, and yet references are made to them everywhere from the Bible to Shakespeare. The symbols of their power are blazoned forth in Every Great House of England and hidden in the Secrets of Freemasonry. These mysteries are not of a God but of a Goddess. The rituals of Nuit Queen of The Stars.

There is no God but Man!

All the secrets of Magick and Alchemy are held by and explained by her.

It is stated in Al, "Solve the first half of The Equation leave the second unattacked". We intend to reveal the second half of The Equation, that of TIME, so that any magickian may be a member of the body of The Silver Star if he so wishes.

It is your function as the chosen ones of AL to weild the power of Thelema instead of being bystanders and saying to your brothers "I told you so" every time something Thelemic happens to the world. It is the duty of every magickian to help humanity in its first tentative steps towards civilisation.

There are many wizards and sorcerers in Thelema who justify their existence by examining the cesspool of creation, the shells and "atavistic resurgences", - I did it myself in my younger days. Pouring minutely through the dunghill of creation is quite entertaining. You can invent bogey men and literally

7 2

All the demons and monsters of the deeps can be yours. You can convince yourself that down is up and give credence to these shells as valid entities. They will conspire with your vanity and claim to teach you great secrets, but the suspicious thing about them is that they never seem quite able to come up with a complete story, and the wisdom they impart is always incomplete, because they are in the process of disintegration. How then can one expect to get a complete truth from them? They represnt old computer programmes, they are old and outworn, but would gladly fasten on any occultist who would give them credence and thus a little more life. I would conjure you to treat them in the way another great master treated them - love them utterly, consume their devils, demons, monsters, call them what you will - love them with the divine love that is over law and help them release the energy they are holding locked up, so that this energy can be used for other forms that are more amusing to the magickian.

The Thelemic movement has been a house divided against itself. Its leaders picking over the grave of Aleister Crowley for would be relics and bits of paper to prove their various rights of succession, but who cares? In the class A publications we have a magick and philosophy of life to use and live by for the next 2,000 years. I suggest that all the various factions forget their differences and get rid of their petty old Aeon attitudes so that we may get on with the work that the Cosmic Secret of the A∴A∴ may be wedded to the terrestial secret that has been revealed by the O.T.O. and the magick of Thelema may at last start ruling the world consciously. Do what thou wilt shall be the whole of the law and Love is the law, love under will.

VOLUME 5 PART 3. 1981.

Editorial

&

The Key to the English Qaballa by Carol A. Smith
(aka Jim Lees)

editorial

This number of The Journal and those to follow will be limited
to 250 copies each signed by the Editors. The information presented in this Vol. of the Journal contains details of secrets
that have remained in the Sanctuaries of initiated occult
orders for Centuries and only now through these pages are
they seeing the light of Day. The design on the Front Cover is
a talisman of Apochryphon that seals our Journal from the
profane.Each Journal is a declaration of The Certainty of Nuit
and whose fate is as certain as Liber Al vel Legis.

To invoke The Elixir of Life into one's being is one thing but
to invoke the powers of the Aeon at the same time is extremely
dangerous even for an initiate.The Astrological configurations
occuring in April 1981 cause these two powers to unite

$$\odot \; \sigma \; ♀ \; \sigma \; \sigma \; ♂ \qquad \mathbb{D} \; \sigma \; ♀ / ♂$$

making scarlet The Goddess and she will manifest in her most
destructive form - so beware. Although destructive the power
invoked clears the way for the Red Elixir to act infinitely
when properly prepared.

The articles on E Q and its Thelemic magick of The Stars is no
tea party magic it is The Magick of The Aeon and manifests the
power of the 93 Current, so unless you are ready to enter the
four gates of The Palace you had better leave it alone, & concentrate upon the initiation of the lower grades.Those already
of the grade 5 = 6 will know the law of "The Fortress" and be
capable of preparing the physical Elixir's green white and red.

    SUN + VENUS + MOON = THE LOVELY STAR = IT SHALL NOT FADE
                = THIS LINE DRAWN = 156

We regret the delay in publishing this edition of T.N.E/B.J.M.
but in view of the nature of some of the material it was decided to time it with the triple conjunction of ♃ and ♄.

Jim Lees & Carol A. Smith co-editors.

THE KEY TO THE ENGLISH QABALLA

by Carol A. Smith

Aleister Crowley did not write the Book of the Law - he was the scribe writing under the direction of the praeter-human intelligence Aiwass. That the numerical qaballa which has been revealed in previous articles could not have been devised by any human intelligence is self-evident; however, doubters need a proof that is irrefutable to stir their darkened souls. The Book of the Law furnishes a proof so startling, so clear, so devastatingly simple that no one can deny its truth.

A key has been left by Crowley, under the direction of Aiwass, in order that "Thou shalt obtain the order and value of the English Alphabet". (I.55). The instruction is in Ch. 3 V.47 "This book shall be translated into all tongues but always with the original in the writing of the beast; for in the chance shape of the letters and their position to one another; in these are mysteries no beast shall divine." Fig. 1 is a full size facsimile of the original of the Book of the Law - Sheet 16 of Chapter 3 of Crowley's note paper on which he took down Liber Al. The rest of verse 47 is written out over a grid pattern with an oblique line drawn across it and a rose cross ⊕ symbol near the end of the line. The secret of this page has never before been revealed.

There are letters along the top of the page, and it would seem to be obvious to continue with the alphabet in the manner indicated, but the clue is in the numbers down the side. A is written instead of 1 which suggests that B is 2, C 3 and so on. Fill in all the squares on the grid in this manner (see fig. 2), repeating the alphabet when one gets to Z. To proceed to the next step the instruction is written on the page, for those who have eyes to see "Then this line drawn is a key." The line drawn is a diagonal line across the page. If one reads any diagonal across the square one gets the order of the English alphabet to be used in the English Qaballa. Whichever diagonal is read the order of the letters is obtained (see fig. 3). There is only one order which

109

CHANCE SHAPE OF THE LETTERS AND THEIR POSITION TO ONE ANOTHER:
IN THESE ARE MYSTERIES THAT NO BEAST SHALL DIVINE. LET HIM NOT
SEEK TO TRY: BUT ONE COMETH AFTER HIM, WHENCE I SAY NOT, WHO
SHALL DISCOVER THE KEY OF IT ALL. THEN THIS LINE DRAWN IS A
KEY: THEN THIS CIRCLE SQUARED IN ITS FAILURE IS A KEY ALSO.
AND ABRAHADABRA. IT SHALL BE HIS CHILD & THAT STRANGELY. LET
HIM NOT SEEK AFTER THIS:FOR THEREBY ALONE CAN HE FALL FROM IT.

110

can be obtained and all 26 letters appear in this order. One numbers
all the letters in this order from 1 to 26 and one gets the English
Qaballistic Alphabet thus:-

A	L	W	H	S	D	O	Z	K	V	G	R	C
1	2	3	4	5	6	7	8	9	10	11	12	13

N	Y	J	U	F	Q	B	M	X	I	T	E	P
14	15	16	17	18	19	20	21	22	23	24	25	26

The other method of obtaining the English Qaballa using the key of 11
has been expalined in Vol.5 No.1.Even on this page there is a reference
to it..."Then this line drawn is a key..and Abrahadabra". Abrahadabra
is an eleven lettered word emphasising the elevenfold nature of the key.

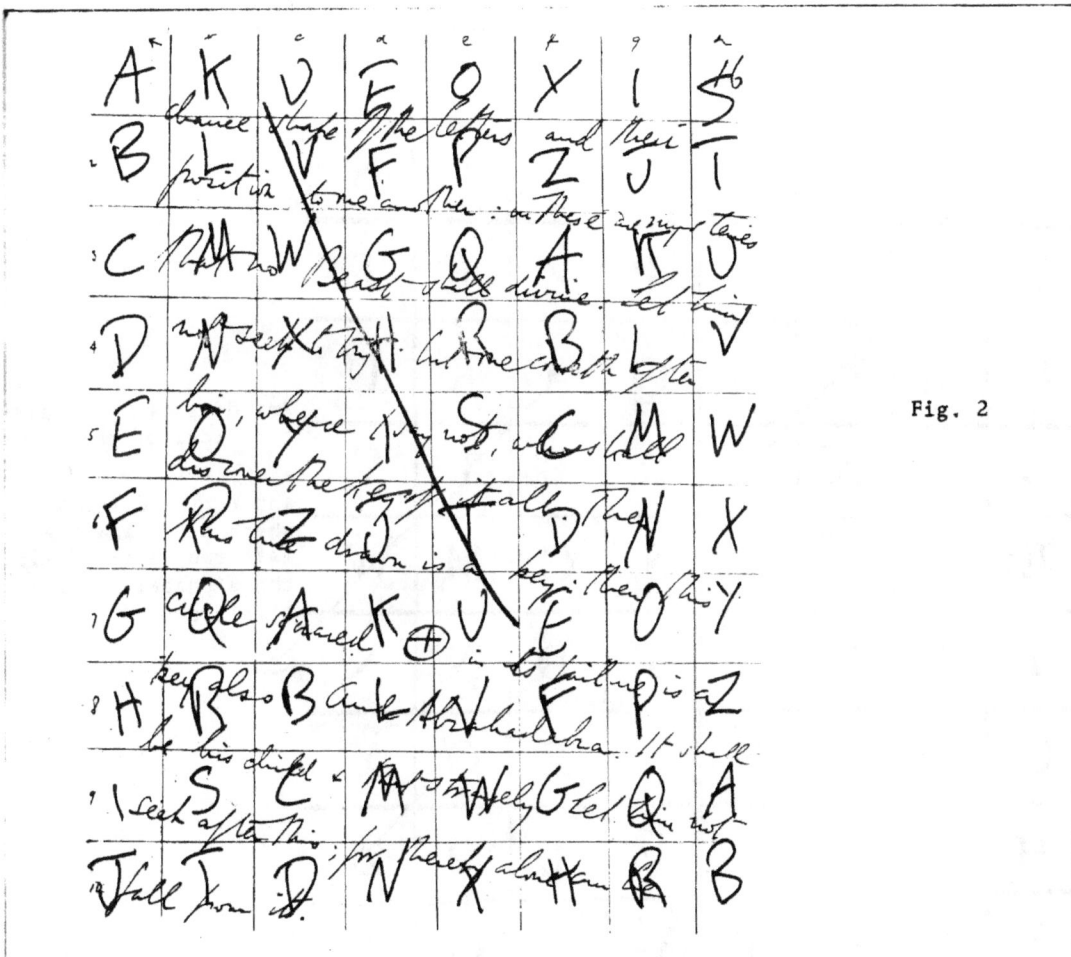

Fig. 2

There is a further mystery. Study the text of the page - the phrase
"whence I say not" occurs in relation to the discovery of the key. The
unconscious mind ignores the concept of "not" for it cannot grasp negative qualities. This factor is well known by advertisers (watch for

111

it) and news reports of the "Mr. Brown is <u>not</u> a homosexual" variety.
Once the concept has been placed, even with a negative, the positive
is what remains. The line drawn and the rose cross symbol bear a
striking resemblance to the area where the key was revealed. The line
drawn is in actuality a permanent way, the circle squared is an area
called "Rosy Cross". No one knows why this area is called Rosy Cross,
for nothing exists there to justify the name.The location of the dis -
covery of the key is in the position "whence" in the manuscript!

So this page of Liber Al not only says there is a hidden key, and
reveals it, but also shows where it will be discovered. This proof is
irrefutable, it is there in black and white for all to see. The gods
which fashioned the Book of the Law, directed the formation of the
English Language, and left a key to its hidden meaning are here, now,
among us all.

SANCTIONED BY FR. P-ACHAD-O 9=2 A.A.

Fig. 3

A	K	U	E	O	Y	I	S
B	L	V	F	P	Z	J	T
C	M	W	G	Q	A	K	U
D	N	X	H	R	B	L	V
E	O	Y	I	S	C	M	W
F	P	Z	J	T	D	N	X
G	Q	A	K	U	E	O	Y
H	R	B	L	V	F	P	Z
I	S	C	M	W	G	Q	A
J	T	D	N	X	H	R	B

Any diagonal will give
the order of the letters
eg ① A L W H S D O Z
and eg② E P A L W ,
where E & P are the
last two letters before
the alphabet repeates
itself again.

VOLUME 5 PART 4. 1981.

Editorial

&

93 The Spell of Nature by Bro. Leo 5 = 6 A∴A∴
(aka James Lees)

editorial

The great God progress is dead - the concept of strict Darw-
inian evolution that supported it is on its knees. We are seeing
the New Aeon manifestations all around us. Mechanistic philosophy
is being superceded by Magical philosophy. The discoveries on the
frontiers of particle physics, molecular biology, and cosmology
all go to support our ethos.

This being so one would expect that a modern Thelemic organisation like the O.T.O. would be brimming with energy - not so
unfortunately.

The O.T.O.s we have investigated are less Thelemic than the
Salvation Army! The only exception is the branch run by Grady
Mc Murtry in California. They have been consistently Thelemic
in their outlook and behavior. All the others seem to have been
thrown out at one time or another by someone or another, with one
exception; and that organisation's sole claim to fame is that it
spends all its resorces on chasing copyright problems. We refrain
from publishing its name in case we are in breach of copyright.

In volume 5 we have among other things described one of the
most incredible phenomenon in modern history - a modern Holy
text which by its Qaballa proves beyond doubt the existance of
the Gods.

We promised to reveal the central secrets of Magick - this
we have done. Some information has been allegorical; for example
the herbal article in this issue. Some information has had to
remain allegorical as a certain occult society has asked that
it be so, and we cannot break faith with them.

Volume 5 has laid the theoretical groundwork of the New
Aeon Magick. In volume six we will consider the use of this magick in Thelemic lodges today, its rituals, spells, and practice
and their practical results in the world. We have given the
theory - in volume 6 we will explain how it is done and what
happens.

Jim Lees & Carol A. Smith co-editors.

93, THE SPELL OF NATURE

BY BRO. LEO 5 = 6 A∴A∴

It was stated by Aleister Crowley that the Book of the Law was dictated to him by a praeter human intelligence – his Holy Guardian Angel Aiwass, and the whole thing took place at an unspecified location in Cairo in 1904. Unspecified because Crowley claimed he could not remember where he was at the time! A man who could play three games of chess blindfold simultaneously with three different people could not remember where he was when the greatest book ever written was dictated to him by an Angel!

The Book of the Law is a Class A publication of the A∴A∴. That means that not so much as the style of a letter can be changed because it was thought that even Crowley did not understand all that was written therein. The A∴A∴ under the leadership of Crowley spent many years trying to fathom the mysteries hidden in the Book of the Law and the other Class A publications, but as it says in Al, one would come after him and he would not find the key or understand its mysteries.

III 47   "This book shall be translated into all tongues: but always with the original in the writing of the beast; for in the chance shape of the letters and their position to one another: in these are mysteries that no beast shall divine. Let him not seek to try: but one cometh after him, whence I say not, who shall discover the key to it all."

I 54   "Change not as much as the style of a letter; for behold thou, O prophet, shall not behold all these mysteries hidden therein."

145

Aleister Crowley died in 1947: even this was predicted by the Qaballa.

1 61   ".......ye shall gather goods and store of women and spices;
              ye shall exceed the nations of the earth in splendour &
              pride but always in the Love of me, and so shall ye come
              to my joy."
              1947 by English Qaballa.
              Aleister Crowley died in 1947 aged 72.

He never found the key to the Book, nor did he behold the mysteries hidden therein. It was left to the child mentioned in Al to find the Key, The English Qaballa, and reveal the mysteries that were hidden within the texts of the Class A publication. It is not possible to reveal all the mysteries hidden in Liber Al vel Legis - The Book of the Law, within these pages nor is it lawful. The only Class A comment to Liber Al is the comment written by Ankh Af Na Khonsu and it quite categorically states that each must study it for himself. So we must comply with this rule except to reveal the mystery of the number 93. This number more than any has come to mean The Law of Thelema. Such expressions as "The 93 current" indicate this.

93 is the value of Thelema in Greek Qaballa and as the Al says it is the word of the Law. What is the significance of this number and why is it so important? There are many references to this number in Al and yet few give a clue as to its working. To find the meaning of 93 we have to look at the Stars. Study The Equinox VI No.3, The Treasure House of Images. There are many references in Al to the Stars, but very few magickians have followed the instructions; they preferred to assume that Star meant the wheels or Chakras of Hindu mysticism. I suspect they preferred this because they were not magickians at all but mystics and knew little of the magick of the Stars. However, in Liber 393, a document in Class B with a Class A introduction, is a complete set of adorations to the Zodiac. The only Star symbol that adds to 93 is the sign SCORPIO. This sign is the ruler of the house of death in the Zodiac and has many other interesting meanings. Scorpio has intrigued astrologers for years because of a peculiar fact. <u>When the Moon enters Scorpio nothing can be predicted.</u> Any enterprise begun in Scorpio is doomed to fail. This fact is easily

checked: simply look in an Ephemeris for the current year and find
when the Moon is transitting through Libra-Scorpio and watch events
at that time - they will all come to nothing. On an international
scale, the Cuba Crisis was started with the Moon in Scorpio, as was
the recent attempt to overthrow the Spanish government. - They both
came to nothing.

To find out the meaning of 93 we must look more closely at the Zodiac
again. Zodiac = 58 = Hadit and Hadit is contained within the body
of the Goddess, the Queen of the Stars, Nuit - A Woman. If Hadit
is the parts that go to make up the body of Nuit then the circle of
the Zodiac is she. "I am everywhere the centre as she the circumference
is nowhere found." She is symbolised by the circumference of an
infinite circle. Remember that it is a Goddess - a woman - of whom
we are talking. Let us examine the most important factor of woman
- her reproductive cycle and see if it relates to the Zodiac.

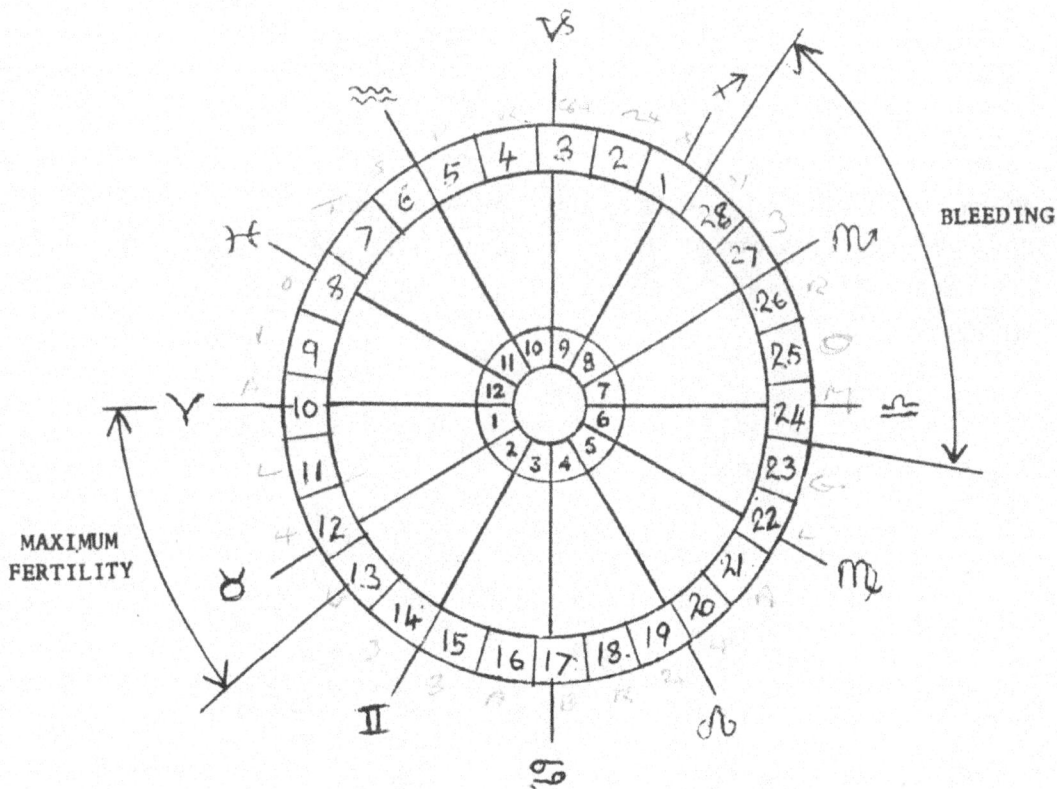

The sex organs are traditionally ruled by Libra and Scorpio. Death/
Scorpio again! It takes approximately 12 days for the moon to get
from Scorpio - the menstrual bleed - to the period of her greatest
fertility - Aries/Taurus. The end (Libra/Scorpio) is the period of

147

harvest, and the maximum fertility (Aries/Taurus) is the time of planting in nature. At least this is so in the country of the language in which Al was written, England and English. The Zodiac then follows the reproductive cycle of Nature (= 93) and the reproductive cycle of woman - The Goddess Nuit.

It would seem that we have wandered far from the point, the number 93, but this is not so, for the menstrual cycle in woman and the apparent death of Nature both have the same symbol, Scorpio, and Nature and Scorpio both have the same numerical value - 93 - whereas Zodiac, Hadit and the sign Libra = 58 = The Secret Seed.

The Seed of Hadit dies in Scorpio; it is expelled during the menstrual flux - anything started at this time will come to nothing. Any seed, idea or enterprise hegun during the 93 period will fail. But where is all this leading us? It is said in Liber 393, The Treasure House of Images, that Scorpio is the formula of unity through denial: anything started during this period will be denied. The initiates of old knew this formula when they went into a fast during this period and wore sackcloth and ashes and lived in and lamented their poverty. If they did this during 93 this would be denial, then they could not be poor, but would be surrounded by opulence. The Templars knew this when they performed their obscene and destructive rites during the 93 periods; they knew that their sin would bring them to the light, as after this period Sin would be denied them by the Zodiac or Nature.

To those who have the simple keys of alchemical art the way to make gold from the base metals is obvious.

Whatever one expects during 93 will not happen. This was the most explosive magickal formula of the ages and was hidden behind myths and symbols throughout the Ages and only now is it being revealed to the Abasement of the Eighties. Look at the hideous god of the Templars again - Baphomet: he turns into the beautiful god with the movement of the hands of a clock! There are many 93 periods in the Zodiac besides the lunar passage through Scorpio, the greatest one being at the conjunction of the Sun with Venus: the time when the Sun takes all the power of the Goddess with the sign of the celestial pentagram. (See BJM/TNE Vol. V No. 3 for a resume of this formula).

It is said in the gnostic gospels repeatedly by Christ that one must study nature if the mysteries are to be revealed to one. Study Nature. Nature = 93 and natural = 71 = Venus. Hidden within Liber Al are all the hidden secrets of Nature and of Magick. They are concealed in the text and revealed by number to give the magickal formula of the eternal circle of the Goddess.

We have only mentioned one of these formulae to comply with the "Each for himself" command of Ankh-Af-Na-Khonsu. We can do little more except indicate the ways in which The Qaballa of Al is used at the present day by A∴A∴ initiates. Those same initiates who have been commanded to help humanity in its first tentative steps towards civilisation in this the aftermath of the Equinox of the Gods: the Equinox that has left mankind reeling and shattered at the speed with which the old Aeon values are being torn apart and discarded: the Equinox that brought two world cataclysms and led man finally to understand that wars were no longer allowed as a means of seeling conflicts between nations.

The Thelemite who works with the Book and its Qaballa will be infallibly led to the citadel of God and in his hands will be given all the keys to magick - the keys to life and death.

THE NEW EQUINOX

THE BRITISH JOURNAL OF

MAGICK

The quarterly occult review of all aspects of **MAGICK**

In-depth articles   reviews   innovatory magical research

Privately circulated material formerly available only to initiates

Available from Kaaba Publications

12A Albert Road, Tamworth, Staffs, England

Price £1.50 + 20p post & packing (US & Canada $5.)

VOLUME 6 PART 1. 1981.

Editorial

&

A Commentary on the 418/II:76 Monograph
by Bro. Leo 5 = 6 A∴A∴
(aka Jim Lees)

&

The Minor Adept Formula of the A∴A∴
by Carol A. Smith
(aka Jim Lees)

EDITORIAL

The birth pangs of the New Aeon are causing problems everywhere.
Politicians and Sociologists have got no idea how to cope with
it. They see the work ethic dying and in a lot of cases taking
its proponents with it. The whole of the Western world is on
the borders of civilisation. The dark ages of the slave religions are ending and the magickal aeon of the crowned and
conquering child is with us. All the Thelemic predictions are
coming true. The magicians have been right all along, and we
have to light the way for the less fortunate of humanity. Thelema
is the future of the world; there are no choices. The formulae of
'Do what thou wilt shall be the whole of the law' and 'Love is the
law, love under will' will be the norm for the world in thirty
years, or there will be no world at all! Thelemites are truly
kings among kings - they know the future; it is up to us to share
our knowledge.

People of all English speaking countries may raise themselves in
pride knowing that it is their language that is the magickal
formula of the Aeon. English will eventually conquer the world.
It will not be America's military might that will eventually
rule the world but her language. The New Aeonic Language of
Thelema.

Volume VI of The New Equinox/British Journal of Magick is
dedicated to the practical aspects of the system. We will give
you the formulae to forge the sword of Thelema. These mighty
secrets are concealed by word and revealed by number. Using the
English Qaballa as the key the cosmology of the twin trees has
been worked out.

JIM   LEES   &   CAROL A. SMITH
(co-editors)

A COMMENTARY ON THE 418/2:76 MONOGRAPH

BY BRO. LEO 5 = 6 A∴A∴

In the following article we are going to discuss many problems that have confounded Thelemic magickians since 1904. To verify our conclusions we have used English Qaballa and we have kept this to a bare minimum. However, one must use Qaballa if the magickian is to survive the highways and byways of modern magick. The Qaballistic confirmation of our conclusions fills the class A material; indeed The Book of the Law is a commentary on the intercourse and transactions that occur between the two Trees of Life indicated by II 76. It is not possible to give all these formulae in such a short treatise: therefore, we hope the reader will bear with us in our limited exposition.

There are many systems of magic, one suited to one individual, another to another, and most of them work, but this is the end of the road for Sorcerers, Witches and Wizards, and the beginning of the Royal Road of Thelema. The magician is like a child picking up stones on a seashore, to misquote Newton. The magickian is the same child, now grown, setting sail on the great sea in search of his destiny and his homeland - to heal the division that is "hither homeward".

Many are the ordeals he must suffer on his way to the truth Absolute and upon his return from his long journey he returns in silence as its Lord and as Harpocrates he rules the world, a silent witness to the Glory of the Star.

This article reveals the compass setting and the charts the magickian must use in his voyage beyond the seashore of eternity.

10

LIBRA + SCORPIO + SAGITTARIUS + CAPRICORN = 418
AYE LISTEN TO THE NUMBERS & THE WORDS = 418
      93   200

1st Consideration

The number 93 is the value of the word of the law, Thelema, in Greek. The word listen combined with the word of the law suggests that this word of the law must be heard in connection with THE NUMBERS (and) THE WORDS = 200 = MANIFESTATION.

MANIFESTATION = 200: this is any form of manifestation and is not subject to the law of Thelema 93. To make manifestation obey Thelemic law its word must be made to obey the law.

2nd Consideration

The word LISTEN = 93 implies that this formula must be applied to the next section. The problem of II 76 has puzzled Thelemites since the book was received in 1904. It is a series of numbers and letters that have defied interpretation by several generations of magicians and scholars, indeed it is claimed by the leaders of Thelemic cults the world over that he or she who solves this peculiar equation shall be the "Chief of All" predicted by Al, such was the importance placed upon this strange verse.

If we apply English Qaballa to II 76 we get

4 6 3 8 ABK 24 A	LGMOR 3 YX	(24) (89) RPSTOVAL
58 Libra	93 Scorpio	200 Manifestation

As the reader will know from previous articles on 93 this number represents the menstrual flux in woman, Scorpio; the whole formula being:-

LIBRA + SCORPIO + SAGITTARIUS + CAPRICORN = 418 EQ

This gives the correspondences shown in the table on the next page.

3rd Consideration

THE NUMBERS + THE WORDS = (24) (89) RPSTOVAL = 200 = MANIFESTATION

11

SUBJECT	LIBRA 58	SCORPIO 93	SAGITTARIUS 14 6	CAPRICORN 121
Magickian Sun conjunct Venus	candidate	The Ordeal X	Integration	Thelemite
Woman	Unfertilised seed	Menstrual flux	Rest	Renewed Woman
Christ	Judgement	Crucifixion (mysteries of the crucifixion = 418)	Mysterious 3 days	Resurrection
Christian	Sin v Self	Repentance	Redemption	Christian
Nature	Harvest	Apparent death of Nature	Rest	Green Man — potential for renewal
Mind	World/Ego conflict	Neurosis	Breakdown. Upsurge of unconscious forces	Catharsis
Existence	Life	Death	Rest	Rebirth
Evolution	Evolutionary stasis	Conversion of species	Consolidation of adaption	New variety
Science	Problem	Intense study	Rest	Solution
Nations	Conflict	War (negotiations)	Agreement Armistice	Peace
Health	Disease	Treatment	Rest	Renewal
Day	Activity	Onset of sleep	Rest	Renewal
Mystic	Illumination	Dark night of the soul	Realisation	Prophet
Thelemite	Names enemy in Libra/Scorpio	Enemy cast into 93	Silence	Free of enemy
Magickian 5 = 6	Names all the things he does not want — enemies	Enemies are destroyed, leaving space in experience and consciousness	Space taken up by "What the enemies are not". i.e. that considered advantageous to the Magickian's will.	Will of Magickian fulfilled

Apply the word of the law to manifestation, that is add 93 to every character in (24) (89) R = 12, P = 26, S = 5, T = 24, O = 7, V = 10, A = 1, L = 2 and we get the following numbers

117:182:105:119:98:117:100:103:94:95:

There are ten characters in this equation, as there are ten characters in the Libra section. If we apply the same rules to the Libra section we get

97:99:96:101:94:113:102:95:97:94

The number 58 = HADIT = LIBRA. In the Book of the Law HADIT says he is perfect (I am perfect being 93 not etc.) and Libra is the sign of The Balance, a further indication of this fact of

12

perfection.   Summarising, we have two sets of ten characters divided by LGMOR 3 YX = 93.   "I am divided (DIVIDE = 93) for love's sake" I.29 Al.   Later in I.30 is PAIN OF DIVISION = 200 = MANIFESTATION.   The method that zero uses to manifest is the Tree of Life.   Therefore, we have two Trees of Life divided by 93 LGMOR 3 YX. (see diagram)

The Libra Hadit Tree is perfect.   Therefore, its Malkuth is placed in Daath to give the perfected Tree.   We have included some of the words in Al that have the values of the various Sephirah to give the reader some idea of what these two Trees mean in terms of Qaballistic symbolism, using English Qaballa, the cipher of the New Aeon.

As will be seen by any Thelemite magickian, this system follows The Book of the Law in its interpretation of manifestation.   Let us consider the myth of creation in Liber Al as given in I.28 (28 = WORD)

```
        NONE BREATHED THE LIGHT FAINT & FAERY OF THE STARS
         60      117      117    80          71
```

On the Tree of manifestation Kether is HOOR-PAAR-KRAAT = 117. Consider this proposition: if None i.e. Zero is Ain Soph then the next word must indicate the number one or Kether.   In this case BREATHED = HOOR-PAAR-KRAAT = THE LIGHT.   None is nothing and NOTHING = RA-HOOR-KHUT = 97, which is the Kether and Yesod of the perfect Tree.   Strictly speaking, NONE = 60 = DEATH (FOR DEATH = 97) and this formula relates to LGMOR 3 YX = 93 = Scorpio, the house of death, but we are discussing II.76 in terms of the Minor Adept's understanding.   The NONE = DEATH formula relates to 8 = 3 and is experienced by the 7 = 3 in his ordeal.

It is impossible to understand The Book of the Law without recourse to the English Qaballa, but those who posess the English Qaballa of Al will see by its numerical commentary the true meaning of existance and the mechanisms of the magick of the New Aeon.

13

ABRAHADABRA
CROWN OF ALL (79)
HEAVEN

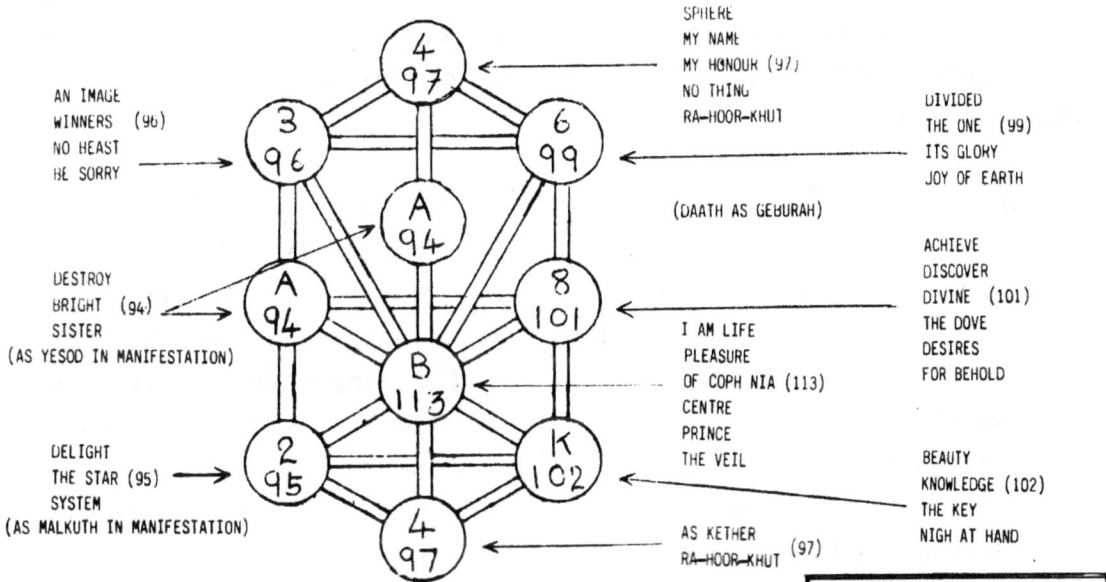

SPHERE
MY NAME
MY HONOUR (97)
NO THING
RA-HOOR-KHUT

DIVIDED
THE ONE (99)
ITS GLORY
JOY OF EARTH

AN IMAGE
WINNERS (96)
NO BEAST
BE SORRY

(DAATH AS GEBURAH)

ACHIEVE
DISCOVER
DIVINE (101)
THE DOVE
DESIRES
FOR BEHOLD

DESTROY
BRIGHT (94)
SISTER
(AS YESOD IN MANIFESTATION)

I AM LIFE
PLEASURE
OF COPH NIA (113)
CENTRE
PRINCE
THE VEIL

DELIGHT
THE STAR (95)
SYSTEM
(AS MALKUTH IN MANIFESTATION)

BEAUTY
KNOWLEDGE (102)
THE KEY
NIGH AT HAND

AS KETHER
RA-HOOR-KHUT (97)

Circles (upper tree): 4/97, 3/96, 6/99, A/94, A/94, 8/101, B/113, 2/95, K/102, 4/97

LGMOR3YX = 93

TIME   BEING   THYSELF   UNITY   DIVIDE (93)

MANIFESTATION = PAIN OF DIVISION = 200

HADIT	
LIBRA	58
HOUSE (58)	+
ORDEALS	93
SIGNS	= 151 = THE HOST

FROM
(OF HEAVEN

CERTAINTY
= LIGHTENING
EIGHTEEN

BLESSING
OBJECT
KNEWEST (105)
NIGHT SKY
CONVERT
OF WORSHIP

MY IMAGE
MYSTERY
LETTERS (117)   HOOR-PAAR-KRAAT
THE LIGHT
RAPTURE
EXPOUND

RESTRICTION (182)
(ABSOLUTE TRUTH PORTAL

SMITE
STRIKE
EATING
EXHAUST (98)
FAILURE
TONGUE

STRENGTH
CREATION
EMBLEMS (119)
DESIRABLE
PROMISE
SPLENDROUS

AS KETHER (117)

ALPHABET
TONGUES
ETERNAL (103)
SPEAKER
SEEING
SMELLING

ADORATIONS
QUEEN
LOVE CHANT
DAUGHTER (100)
LITTLE
HRUMACHIS

COMETH
DEPART
DESTROY (94)
GIRDERS
TRODDEN

SELF-SLAIN
HOLY PLACE
PERISH (95)
SYSTEM
DELIGHT

Circles (lower tree): 24/117, R/105, 89/182, S/98, P/119, T/117, V/103, O/100, A/94, L/95

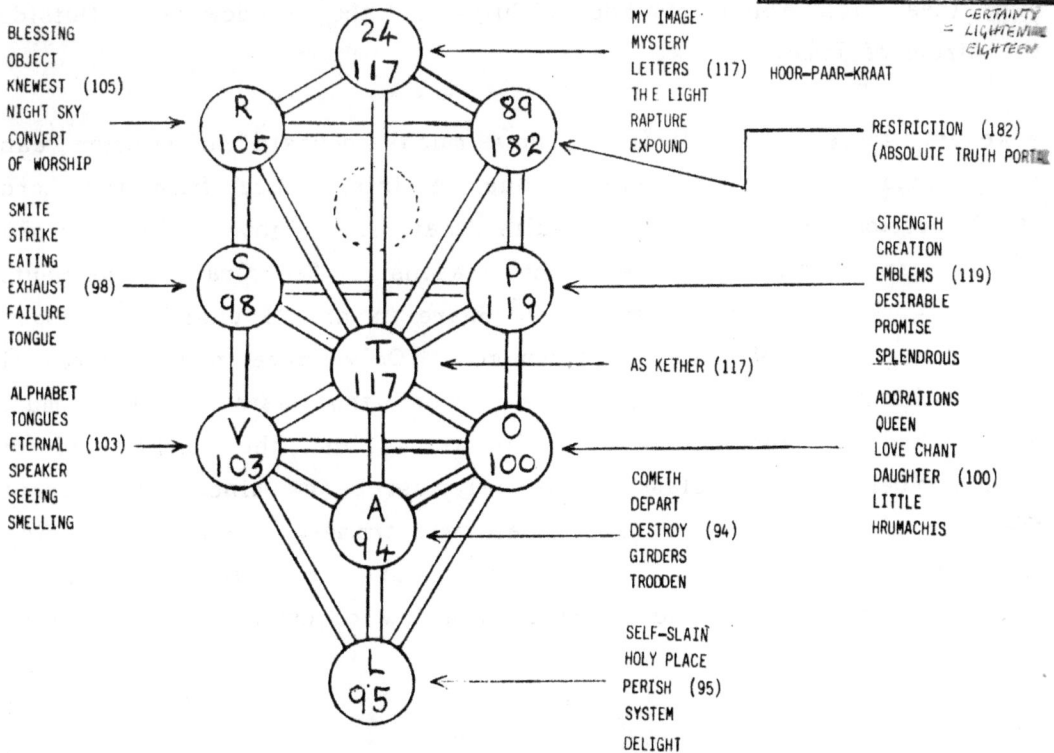

THE QABALLAISTIC EXPOSITION OF CHAPTER II VERSE 76 OF LIBER AL

We have illustrated the action of the 93 formula, using II 76 to reveal how the formula works. It will be seen that Daath and Geburah on the perfect Tree have the same value as Yesod on the Tree of manifestation, as the Hod on the perfect Tree is the same as Malkuth in manifestation. The two Trees are divided by 93. When the stellar configurations are correct, the 93 formula is activated and energy flows out of manifestation to the perfect Tree and vice versa.

In the physical world this results in the appearance of magickal effects and the abortion of Destiny as the perfect Tree adjusts the balance in manifestation. The old concept of only one Tree of Life is impossible as nothing could happen in manifestation beyond the production of the amoeba - a single celled creature. This is obvious, as a Tree going from zero to manifestation could only produce this without periodic interferences from beyond. Look again at the cycle of the Goddess and unite her with manifestation through "Solve et Coagula" and become Baphomet.

Kenneth Grant postulated the existence of two Trees of Life and it is a tribute to this magickian's ability that without the Qaballistic key to Liber Al he produced results that parallel some of our own (see Night Side of Eden, Cults of the Shadow and Outside the Circle of Time).

However, there is a limit to how much accurate information can be gleaned from Astral Contact due to interference from the Lord of Dispersion 93 who gives results that are right for the wrong reasons and wrong for the right reasons. See Grant's comments on the works of Lovecraft and A.O. Spare in his "Typhanian Trilogy" for illustrations of this phenomenon. Only pure numbers reveal the truth and it is against pure number that astral visions must be checked for their validity. It is against the background of pure number that the Class A material must be examined, for without the role of number "these runes" become extremely dangerous, leading one into the minefield of 93. Pure number has always been the way of the magickian, and apart from a few diversions into hallucin-

1 5

ated art and literature.   Anything else is always at best Mysticism and at worst insanity.

<u>418</u>

At the end of chapter II of the Book of the Law it is said "..and the name of thy house 418."

This number by English Qaballa means the "four".   4 are 1 to infinity 8.   The immediate question is what four, and one is inclined to invoke the Lion, Man, Scorpio and Bull as a means of escape from the problem. Yet Leo,Scorpio, Aquarius and Taurus do <u>not</u> add to 418.   In any case this quaternary is not new and in no way represents a revolutionary New Aeon formula.   The New Aeon Quaternary must be revolutionary, not a rehash of old aeon ideas.

This brings us to another question: the phrase refers to THY HOUSE= 101 - whose house are we required to consider?   Reducing the number 1 + 0 + 1 = 2.   the house of duality?   The dual one is Baphomet 128, expressed in the Zodiac as balanced duality CAPRICORN= 121.

The power of Capricorn is derived from Libra, Scorpio, Sagittarius and the value of Libra, Scorpio, Sagittarius and Capricorn is 418 by English Qaballa.   Therefore the house of Baphomet is Libra, Scorpio, Sagittarius and Capricorn.   The next question is why should these signs above any of the rest be worshipped?

We have already given the meaning of 93 Scorpio as the formula of unity by denial that operates when one of the planets or Sun and Moon are in the sign.   During these periods most forms of 93 magick can be performed.   The reason why 418 is of particular interest is that during the Ordeal X the magickian enters the house of Baphomet when the Sun transits these signs.   He enters at Libra, an individual at war with himself and ineffectual in the world, due to this conflict, and leaves at Capricorn, an individual child of Baphomet, able to do his will in the world.   His duality has

16

been reordered to unit through the ORDEAL X = THE BEAST = BAPHOMET = SCARLET WOMAN = 128.

The law of Thelema is the green shoot of spring opening up amongst the death and decay of a defunct Aeon. It is hardly visible, yet it will grow to produce an as yet unknown species of Mankind. A Mankind who will look back on these centuries as the truly dark ages of instinctual man: when men killed each other for illusory gain based upon the idea that it is possible to gain anything in a world in which we have no permanent home. It is as impossible to imagine Thelemic man as it would be impossible for an ape to imagine he could become us.

The promises given in The Book of the Law are no vain promises based upon faith, they are factual statements of our destiny. The third chapter of Al is a statement upon the nature of man. It is often forgotten that Nuit is the goddess who taught discrimination and this virtue is the one most needed in dealing with the Class A material - neglect nothing but remove the husk from the kernel to taste the truth. The husk has been placed there to mislead the unworthy.

The Law of Thelema first integrates and then supersedes all former magical systems. It supersedes them and prepares the way for New Aeon man. This is the way of the future. We are paving the way to the civilisation of the future. There are no choices. The nuclear mad power men of today are in the death throes of their credibility; the future belongs to our successors, the Priests and Priestesses of Thelema. There is no need for dramatic revolution, and violence is for those who would seek to turn back the tide. The Thelemic revolution will happen - is happening naturally.

Everyone who would aspire to Magick will ultimately have to enter the house of Baphomet, through the secret door made for us by our body of the Stars. It is for them that these words are written - the slaves shall serve.

In the next issue of The New Equinox/British Journal of Magick we will reveal the secrets of the enemy naming ceremony and how and why it works.

FROM THE RECORDS OF
G.H. FRATER P-ACHAD-O

17

THE MINOR ADEPT FORMULA

OF THE A∴ A∴

by Carol A. Smith

The function of the A∴A∴ in its present cycle is to teach the Magick of Thelema and the cosmological magick of the New Aeon. It uses as its tool the Class A publications, a cipher code transmitted by the transmundane intelligence Aiwass, and decoded by the English Qaballa. This Magick unites all the known systems of Magic into a coherent whole, thus revealing the true nature of the magic of the distant past and the distant future.

The initiatory process of the A∴A∴ is based upon the stars beginning with the ordeal of the beast. The feast of the Equinox of the Gods is partaken during Sun conjunct Venus. SUN AND VENUS = 128 = THE BEAST = SCARLET WOMAN = BAPHOMET = FIVE WOUNDS. At this time a point of the divine pentagram is made (see The New Equinox/British Journal of Magick Vol.5 No.III). This initiates a process of change within the probationer that continues with the Sun's passage through the Zodiac, and has the nature of the Signs the Sun passes through upon its way to SCORPIO = 93. The universe initiates the candidate. During the process the candidate enters the HOUSE OF BAPHOMET (LIBRA, SCORPIO, SAGITTARIUS, CAPRICORN) = 418. His self and not self are united and he becomes BAPHOMET = 128 or she becomes the SCARLET WOMAN = 128. To perform a ritual synchronised with this stellar configuration causes the candidates to be stripped of all they think about themselves and they are left with two ideas – who they are and who they are not – duality – Baphomet. This produces a confilct in the individual that is resolved around the end of Sun in Sagittarius. The man "dies" and is reborn and when the Sun enters PISCES = RA-HOOR-KHUT he obtains a new identity through the unification of the two aspects of self. This is the NATURE = 93 of the ORDEAL X = 128 = BAPHOMET – the unity 1, of duality 2, to infinity 8. the women in the A∴A∴ are brothers in that they are the Goddess and act upon Man, who is negative in this ordeal.

The duality is reconciled and produces UNITY = 93. His new nature is refined until Sun in Aries when he is able to act on the world as a minor adept of the A∴A∴ and a master of the 93 formula of the Moon. It is not possible to illustrate what the ordeal will be for a given individual, as each will experience it in his or her own very personal way.

The Magick of the New Aeon is not to be undertaken lightly for once the initiatory process in undertaken it cannot be stopped, any more than the stars in their courses. Any person who undertakes to perform the Rosy Cross rite at Sun conjunct Venus has an inviolable right to membership of the A.'.A.'. We refuse none.............It may seem curious to the Magickian that a probationer should pass from such a lowly grade to 5 = 6 in such a short time. In answer to this we say "break the Bar, perform the rite, undergo the ordeal and know!"

The Ordeal X once undergone by a man or woman he or she becomes a Minor Adept of the A.'.A.'. and wields the power of the 93 formula in its lunar aspect and as an initiate of its mysteries cannot be harmed by it as the priest and priestesses of old could not be harmed.

What is the 93 formula in its Lunar phase? To answer this a knowledge of Astrology is required of the reader. During every lunar month the Moon passes through the entire Zodiac. It has been noticed by astrologers that when the Moon hits Scorpio nothing can be predicted successfully. This was put down to unfortunate stars in the constellation of Scorpio. This is the uninitiated view. As was seen in The New Equinox/British Journal of Magick Vol. 5 No.IV, Libra and Scorpio are the signs of the menses in woman, when the unfertilised seed is expelled by the menstruum solvent (Solve et Coagula). In the mundane world whatever is started at this point of the Zodiac will not come to fruition. Anything can happen except that which is expected (the seed). This is easy to check. Simply look up in an ephemeris the time when the Moon is between 15° Libra and 15° Scorpio and watch the progress of events started at this time – they all go wrong.

THE 93 RITUAL OF UNITY BY DENIAL

We cannot give the exact nature of the rite, but we will outline how and why it works. We have said that during 93 the expected never happens. The 5 = 6 organises his ritual in accordance with Liber Al Chapter 3 and the expected future to the adept in the rite is terrible. He names his enemies by writing them on hand made paper using the universal solvent as ink and burns the paper, thus killing them FIRE = NUIT = 78. They are the expected future. At no time does he revile his enemies but simply names them. The way of Christ garbled by centuries was similar, when he recommended "love thine enemies". Love them by all means, but during Scorpio when they will be destroyed by the 93 formula.

No other work is required but the candidate may be prompted by his angel to perform exercises consistant with the work. This is the secret of the ages. In the past pantheons this was always the path of initiation. The priests did not perform long Yogic practices – except in India. All systems of magic in the ancient world were stellar based. This is true in the NEW = 42 = STAR aeon.

The A.'.A.'. member takes advantage of natural forces and lives not only in harmony with nature but is part of it – this is the Thelemic way of life. We have shown that there is a time to sow, a time to reap and another time that rules them all – the time of Scorpio – 93.

Thelema is life and life is Thelema. In the New Aeon philosophy is no myopic magic of bygone years or surreal vision of "artists" who cannot stomach reality. Magick through its ordeals brings one closer and closer to our divine origin and as each ordeal is passed so a new gateway opens and the ordeal-earned power flows through and embodies the magickian.

The formula of 93 is practiced by the 5 = 6 until the next period of Sun conjunct Venus, when he again joins his brothers and sisters to perform The Rosy Cross rite and again partakes in The Feast of The Equinox of the Gods. The power of The Star thus continues his initiation of the five wounds and prepates for him a place among the adepts of eternity, the sacred and secret Kings and Queens of the Earth, rulers of the world for all time and through all space ever unto the ages. Amen.

ARTWORK

P.2. Three faces of the Goddess - Sexual Secrets - Hutchinson

P.24. High Priestess of Baphomet - Cath Thompson

P.28&29 "Brother Jukes" - Dave Johnstone, Belfast.

P.31. Crowley in 1943 - Neptune Press

P.34. Girls with sexual aid - Sexual Secrets.

27

www.ingramcontent.com/pod-product-compliance
Lightning Source LLC
Chambersburg PA
CBHW081135090426

42740CB00015BA/2879